MEET MRS. JOB

CAROLYN L. REYNOLDS

Meet Mrs. Job
by Carolyn L. Reynolds

Printed in the United States of America

ISBN 1-594671-39-7

Unless otherwise indicated, Bible quotations are taken from the King James Version.

Information gathered from:
The Holy Bible, King James and Amplified Version.
Everyday life in Old Testament Times, by E. W. Heaton.
Holman Bible Dictionary, General Editor Trent C. Butler, Ph.D..
The Zondervan Pictorial Bible Dictionary, Merrill C. Tenney.
Matthew Henry's Commentary, Matthew Henry, Zondervan.

Xulon Press
www.XulonPress.com

Xulon Press books are available in bookstores everywhere, and on the Web at www.XulonPress.com.

CONTENTS

ACKNOWLEDGMENT

The historical information for this book was gathered from a variety of manuals.

This is my interpretation, after hours of reading and simulating data, what life was like before and during the timeline of Job.

You have the prerogative to accept or reject anything you read in this book.

This is one of those 'as I see it' books.

My understanding of different views and perspectives come from a variety of historians, researchers and authors, and are expressed in this edition.

I am not a feminist, although I'm not sure what's included in the definition, and I'm not an activist. I love to know why and why not of most everything. I search and research to get a clear understanding of what I'm reading.

I pray that you enjoy your visit with Mrs. Job.

FOREWORD

The reason for this book is explained in the dedications. The
need for this book is also examined in the dedications. We all
need to know and come to an understanding that there is significance
in our lives. We all have a future and the journey to that future is our
destiny. We all from time to time live behind the shadows of others
and think we are nobody going nowhere. After reading about Mrs.
Job you will see that you play an important role in the mind of God,
and that you have a lot to offer into the kingdom of God for the good
of mankind just as you are this very moment. Whether you do or do
not get the recognition you feel you deserve, God sees and hears
what you are doing for the kingdom of God. That is what is vital.

If you have slacked down in your participation towards the
work of the Lord, I encourage you to rekindle the fire that you once
had. Do not allow others to pour water on your flame anymore.
Whatever it takes to jumpstart you on the kingdom path again, do it.
It may be fasting or diligently seeking the face of God.

It may be drawing away from the 'in' crowds. We don't have

time to waste thinking about our circumstances or what other people think about us, action is what is needed.

Remember back to the time when you first caught on fire for God. Recall that passion and go forth with all your might.

Don't dwell on the past or on mistakes that may hold you back, but embrace the lessons learned from them and allow God to propel you forth to His destination for you.

His glory can be revealed in you the same way His glory was revealed in Mrs. Job.

I want to warn you that it will take changing some habits and routines and even behavioral patterns that are comfortable to you. It will take you making a complete turn around in your actions and especially in your thinking (mindset). Renewing your mind will simulate being snatched out of your seat and placed in unfamiliar territory and left alone. Get used to the new views and the new sounds.

Embrace the newness of God's presence.

Seize the moment to charge the atmosphere with praises unto God.

Capture His heart with expressions of love and adoration.

Cause God to come down and inhabit your space with worship unto Him.

DEDICATION

This book is dedicated to all the women who live in the background of their husband's ministry. Your names are rarely mentioned, and you are very seldom acknowledged. You are overshadowed with the crowds that throng around your husband as he humbles himself to the challenge and charge given him. You love the LORD as much as he does, but you understand that even though you both were called, he is the one in the spotlight. When he speaks, all eyes are on him, and frequently on his family to see your response to his statements. You make sure his suits are pressed and cleaned, his shirts spotless, his hair well groomed, his shoes shined, and that he has had proper nutrition for his labor of love schedule. You protect his quiet time, his study time, and his meditation moments. You make sure he is not disturbed during his prayer time, and you honor and respect his seasons of fasting, prayer and solitude.

God has not forsaken you. He has not forgotten you.

This book is also dedicated to all the men that exist in the backdrop of your wives public setting. Most people don't even know that she's married or that she has a family. You sit in the front row encouraging her. But you are not known to anyone else. Especially not known as her husband. When the crowds gather around her, you hang back unnoticed, but close enough to let her know that you support her. When she is introduced you are not mentioned and not even picked up on the monitor when she shares family events. You're accused of being a groupie because of the way you attempt to protect her. It's up to you to make sure the children are properly cared for (school, doctor appointments, athletic practices and games) and the house maintained. You hire the housekeepers and nannies so that your wife can give her very best to and for God. At times you are the secretary, the schedule maker and you see to it that the schedules are kept. You make sure she gets enough sleep and nutrition. You handle family finances and do not bother her with unnecessary (mundane) details.

God has not forsaken you. He has not forgotten you.

Many men and women that are called by God to serve in His ministry, their spouses and families are overlooked as being a significant participator in the success of the men and women of God. There are many times people forget that you exist.

This book is dedicated to all the sons that had to grow up without your father or mother attending your games, school programs or plays. They were not there when your little league team won their first game because of your great pitching ability. When you starred in the school/church play, your babysitter cheered you on. When you had the measles and chicken pox the nanny was there. When you fell off the jungle gym and had to go to the emergency room, your parents were out of town preaching God's Word. They were not there when you received an award for your skill on the debating team.

God has not forsaken you. He has not forgotten you.

This book is dedicated to all the daughters whose mother was not there to share their secrets with and whose father was not around to listen to your problems. When a close friend hurt your feelings, no one was there to explain the seemingly betrayal of friendships. While your mother and father were in the spotlight, you received no attention. No one explained your need for braces, how to be self-confident or how to handle your first infatuation. No one was there to validate you as a person. When you started on your menstruation, you bashfully fumbled through on your own applying the knowledge you gathered during girl talk. Who taught you to rely on God?

God has not forsaken you. He has not forgotten you.

MISCONCEPTIONS ABOUT JOB'S WIFE

I want to introduce you to a woman who lived in the shadow and background of her husband, his prestige and his success. Very little is written and recorded in the Bible about her. The few words she spoke are recorded and not taught that they were words of compassion and understanding.

> *Job 2:9... 'Then said his wife unto him, Dost thou still retain thine integrity? curse God, and die.'*

She sounds as if she is a woman that has no heart for what Job is going through. As a young Christian and all through my maturing years I heard only negative comments preached and proclaimed about the wife of Job. I finally realized that if I really wanted to know the character of Job's wife, I had to see her through the character of Job himself.

The Bible relates in great detail about the character and

integrity of Job. We know that he was perfect and upright, and that he feared (loved and reverenced) God, and eschewed evil (***Job 1:1***). We know about his travail and how he cursed his birth (***Job 3:1-4***). We understand his sufferings and his loss's. There is so much written and recorded about Job, I began to wonder what kind of woman would he marry. I couldn't find much written about her. I reasoned within myself that a man of such excellence and distinction must have a help meet (fit) for him.

I've searched other Bible translations of the book of Job to see if there was anything different written than what the King James Version recorded. Amplified Old Testament... ***'Then his wife said to him, Do you still hold fast your blameless uprightness? Renounce God and die!'***

I read the english words recorded under each Hebrew character in the Interlinear Bible; ***'Then said to him his wife, you still (Are) holding fast to your integrity? Bless God and die!'***

There was one translation/version I read about Mrs. Job's response to her husband's dilemma, which I will share with you in a later chapter.

KNOWN FACTS ABOUT JOB

Job 1:1,8... 'There was a man in the land of UZ, whose name was Job; and that man was perfect and upright, and one that feared God, and eschewed evil.'

Yes, Job was a perfect and upright man, he feared/loved God and eschewed (avoided, hated) evil. God Himself repeated this more than once in the book of Job.

I want to make it very clear that I am not knocking Job. I am not trying to take anything away from Job. When God has spoken His view on the person, who am I to say otherwise. My attempt is to bring light to Mrs. Job, who I believed had a significant role in the life of Job.

Job was the son of *Issachar (Genesis 46:13)... 'And the sons of Issachar; Tola, and Phuvah, and Job, and Shimron.*

Job was the grandson of Jacob and Leah *(Genesis 35:23)... 'The sons of Leah; Reuben, Jacob's firstborn, and Simeon, and*

Levi, and Judah, and <u>Issachar</u>, and Zebulum:' he had a rich heritage.

Job was a righteous man. God attested to that in *Ezekiel 14:14 'Through these three men Noah, Daniel, and <u>Job</u>, were in it, they should deliver but their own souls by their righteousness, saith the Lord GOD.'*

Job was a patient man *James 5:11... 'Behold, we count them happy which endure, Ye have heard of the patient of <u>Job</u>, and have seen the end of the Lord; that the Lord is very pitiful, and of tender mercy.'*

Job was a man of distinction. *1Chronicles 7:5a... 'And their brethren among all the families of <u>Issachar</u> were valiant men of might,'* so Job was a valiant man of might.

Job had understanding of the times; *1 Chronicles 12:32 'And of the children of <u>Issachar</u>, which were men that had understanding of the times, to know what Israel ought to do;'* so Job was a wise man, a man of wisdom. Job was in the generation that had understanding of the times and seasons. He could make wise decisions for God's people and make God's message relevant to people's lives.

Job's wealth was astounding. Job was a man of nobility. His ancestry was from royalty and he amassed quite a fortune on his own.

Job sat in the gate to the city where honorable men, and men of prestige gathered.

Job was considered a judge. He was not one of the 12 men and women hero's included in the book of Judges that delivered Israel from her oppressors.

The wisdom and knowledge that Job possessed qualified him to settle controversies, give opinions and/or decide on the relative worth of anything.

He would be one to whom townspeople would consult about business affairs.

Job understood his gifts, duties and obligations to his God, his nation and his people.

Getting to know the character of Mrs. Job, it will seem as though this book speaks more about Job than his wife. I had to take this route to understand what kind of woman, wife, mother, and companion she was.

THE WORTH OF JOB

Job 1:1… 'There was a man in the land of Uz, whose name was Job; and that man was perfect and upright, and one that feared God, and eschewed evil.'

Job 1:2… 'And there were born unto him seven sons and three daughters.'

Job fathered ten children, but he did not give birth to those children.

Job 1:3… 'His substance also was seven thousand sheep,'

Sheep were kept for their milk more than for their flesh. Sheep were prominent animals used in the sacrificial system. The common breed could store a vast amount of fat in the tail, sometimes weighting as much as 15 pounds and used for food. Sheep were sheared each year to make wool for rugs, blankets, tarpaulin, clothing, wraps, shawls, robes, tunics, loincloths and waist cloths.

Shepherds to tend 7,000 sheep. I'm not sure how many sheep make one flock, but I suppose there were many flocks. An adequate amount of men to shear the sheep. Men and women to weave and spin the wool.

Rams (male sheep) horns were used as trumpets (*Joshua* 6:4), and for carrying oil

(*1 Samuel 16:1*), and as trumpets for summoning the people and in other festivals. The skins of rams (male sheep) were used in making the covering of the tabernacle.

Job must have cornered the fabric and clothing manufacturing market. Even the tentmakers would contact him for textiles. Since Job was a man of extreme wealth and influence, it is likely that he was difficult to locate.

'and three thousand camels'

As beasts of burden, camels could carry about four hundred pounds and travel in caravans covering about thirty miles per day.

Camel's hair woven into a textile was used for coarser cloths to be made into tents, bags, sackcloths and heavy cloaks for shepherds/herdsmen.

Camels were used for long distance travel and communication.

Servants to care for 3,000 camels.

In today's setting Job's camels would compare to A T&T, International News Business, New York Times, Washington Post, CNN. Job had what we call a Fortune 500 Business.

'and five hundred yoke of oxen,'

Oxen are in the cattle family. Oxen provided not only food and animals for sacrifice, but they were also draft (work) animals. A yoke is two, which means he had 1,000 oxen. Oxen were used to till the land and plow the field. He was a major farmer, what we would call a major super market chain. Probably a multi-million dollar business, like Meijer's, Krogers, Farmer Jacks and Piggly Wiggly.

Servants to tend 1,000 oxen.

Today he would be compared to Donald Trump and Bill Gates.

'and five hundred she asses,'

Asses were used as saddle animals, being preferred by rulers and great men for peaceful journeys. Asses were also more sure-footed on mountain trails than horses. Female donkeys were used for short distance travel. They were ridden only by the very elite, the upper class, the wealthy, the rich. Jesus rode into Jerusalem on an ass. (*Matthew 21:1-11*)

Servants to be responsible for 500 she asses.

Today they would be compared to the Cadillac, Rolls Royce and Lexus Limousine Service.

'and a very great household;'

Servants to tend the oxen and the asses; shepherds/herdsmen, servants and shearer's for the sheep; servants to care for the camels; maids and servants for the children.

> *'so that this man* (**Job**) *was the greatest of all the men of the east.'*

Job 1:4... 'And his sons went and feasted in their houses, every one his day; and sent and called for their three sisters to eat and to drink with them.'

Their children were grown, seeing they owned real estate, had family gatherings, often.

(Who raised and nurtured the sons and daughters of Job to a mature age?)

For Job and his household to be so grounded in family values, it speaks volumes about Mrs. Job. He was building an empire, so his time was very limited in the home.

The balance of chapter one in the Bible records in details the fate of Job's empire. Chapter 2 begins with Job being tested again.

Now there is no doubt in our minds that Job had a solid and personal relationship with God. He loved God with all his heart. He did all the godly and right things to stay in covenant with God. Job understood his imperfections and sacrificed at the family altar to atone for his and his families' shortcomings. Job never charged God foolishly after all that happened to him. Job continued to worship God even in his affliction.

What about Mrs. Job? We read one verse of her response to the entire situation, and it seemed not to be a compassionate concern.

JOB'S CALAMITIES

The demise of Job was great. Only a person who loves the LORD and practices a deep relationship with Him would be found still standing (believing in the grace and mercy of God) in the midst of all the disaster that Job experienced.

> *Job 1:14,15... (paraphrase) 'And the Sabeans fell upon the oxen and the asses, took them away and slain the servants with the edge of the sword.'*

Seba, the son of Raamah, the son of Cush (*Genesis 10:7; 1 Chronicles 1:9*) were known as the Sabeans (descendents of Noah). They were also known as travelling or nomadic merchants. There was one witness spared to carry a message to Job to tell him of what all had happened.

His grocery store chain and his limousine service was gone.

What liability did Job have in place for the widows and families of the servants (none were listed as slaves) that tended his oxen and asses?

Job 1:16... (paraphrase) 'fire fell from heaven and consumed all the sheep and shepherds/servants except one.'

Job's milk supply, his source for animal sacrifice, his supply of horns for trumpets; his rams skins trade was all gone. His fabric and clothing business (designer shops) was shut down. His entire textile empire went up in smoke.

How many shepherds and servants homes were left with no source of support?

Job 1:17... (paraphrase) 'the Chaldeans stole the camels and slain the servants, except one to report the disaster.

Job lost another part of his textile business. The coarser fabric made from the camel's hair could not be produced. This was a big part of making tents, sackcloth and heavy cloaks for shepherds. Long and short distance travel and communication, for the Jobs' was at a standstill.

Animal handlers/trainers and maintenance/groomers wives, sons and daughters left with no one to care for them. One servant survived to deliver the news.

Job 1:18,19... (paraphrase) 'a great wind from the wilderness smote the four corners of one of the sons house where they were eating and drinking (birthday party- Amplified version) and they were all killed. Only one servant escaped to tell the news.'

All of Job's children died that day. Not one child survived the tragedy.

One messenger was left to tell of the grave adversity.

Job 2:7... 'So went Satan forth from the presence of the LORD, and smote Job with sore boils from the sole of his foot unto his crown. And he took him a potsherd to scrape himself withal; and he sat down among the ashes.'

Job's entire body was riddled with erysipelas (Matthew Henry Commentary), an acute infectious disease of the skin or mucous membrane caused by a streptococcus and characterized by local inflammation and fever (Webster's Dictionary).

MEET MRS. JOB
A REMARKABLE WOMAN
FULL OF COURAGE AND
INTEGRITY

Job 1:1

Job being a man of nobility and royal ancestry would marry a woman with the same social standing.

In Old Testament times the bridegroom's parents formally arranged marriages.

Job's family was of affluence and greatness, and they would have stayed in their circle of aristocracy when choosing a wife for him.

It is only befitting for a king to marry a princess. It is befitting the dignity of a king's kid to have the very best. It would be only appropriate and right that a man of nobility and of royal descent to marry a woman of distinction and quality.

Job's wife would have been of nobility and wealth.

Even though Jacob met Rachel at a well and fell in love with her at first sight *(Genesis 29:10,11,18)*, and agreed to work seven years for her, that was not the normal procedure of a marriage arrangement.

Job's parents would have been very careful to choose an acceptable match for him.

She would be a refined woman, an equal to his status and standing in society. She must have been attractive because her second set of daughters were the fairest in all the land *(Job 42:15)*.

Job 1:2

Even thought Job had 10 children, he did not give birth to those children.

Up to this time Mrs. Job had been pregnant 90 months of her life.

That equals to 7 ½ years of her body being pushed out of shape.

The organs inside her body were rearranged 10 times and probably not the same rearrangement each time. We know that each pregnancy is different.

How was her health during each 9-month period?

Was each pregnancy free of morning sickness, or headaches?

Did her body retain water and her feet swell?

Was each delivery free of complications?

For each pregnancy, who took care of the already born children?

Mrs. Job had the physical capacity to carry those children.

It was her birth canal that they came through.

It was the milk in her breast that fed them.

It was Mrs. Job that went through deaths doorway 10 times in child delivery.

Mrs. Job gave birth to those 10 children.

While Job was building his empire, Mrs. Job was birthing and raising children.

Job was not always away. With 10 children he spent some time at home.

In that culture there were fatherly duties and obligations to his family that he must perform.

I'm sure Job brought some wealth into his marriage, but to accumulate such a fortune he was a man of vision. It was not uncommon for a man of royalty and wealth to have more than one wife. I don't remember mention of more than one wife for Job. The birth of a child interrupted the daily routine of the mother. I'm sure there were midwives, nannies and nurses.

It was customary to breast feed babies until the child is two to three years old.

It is difficult to become pregnant while you are still breast-feeding. That is a fact known even today. So we may conclude that Mrs. Job's children were at least 2 to 3 years apart. She was a busy lady.

Because of the Job's royal and wealthy status in life, Mrs. Job must have had nannies and servants at her disposal. There was a weeklong celebration (party) every time a child was born, and when the baby was weaned, another party. Mrs. Job was the center of attention in her home.

The development of character in a child takes the nurturing of male and female, both parents.

Mr. and Mrs. Job both took part in educating their children.

For the first few years of their lives, boys and girls were brought up by their mothers. Later the boys would be transferred to their fathers.

Mrs. Job would make sure that learned and compassionate men were included in the staff teaching the boys when Job was not there.

Mrs. Job would see to it that the children were potty trained (no pampers no potty-chairs). She may not have done the chore personally, but she would be certain that it was done.

She would be the one at home to see that the children were taught good morals and Christian values.

I don't remember reading in the Bible about childhood diseases, there must have been, but in today's setting she would nurture them (comfort all 10 of them) through fevers, ear aches, tooth aches, falls, scrapes and breaks and settle disputes.

Even with our modern day inoculations, there are child sicknesses to deal with.

Mrs. Job would have taken charge of their formal education.

The Jewish community had the opportunity to receive religious education from the priests (Job was the priest of his home) and Levites (religious teachers of the nation). The main purpose among the Jews was the learning of and obedience to the laws of God in words and example.

Generally the boys would be taught a trade, care of the home, and the application of dietary laws. The girls would be taught how to be good wives and mothers.

Children of promise would not be taught generally, but specifically and precisely.

Mr. and Mrs. Job both being from families of affluence would have been taught specific subjects.

Their children, being seeds of substance they would also be taught about their duties and obligations as men and women to their God, their nation and their servants.

Education was also for learning the aspects of everyday life.

The home was the most effective place in processing education and the parents (the Jobs') were considered the most effective teachers to their children, along with the Levites.

The children would have been taught about the feast and observance of the holy days and the significance of them. They would learn about the system of sacrificing.

God charged Abraham, father of God's chosen people, with the responsibility of training his children and his household (the nation of Israel) to walk in the ways of the Lord (***Genesis 18:19***). The training was imparted through conversation, example, and imitation.

Mrs. Job would oversee all these aspects of the children's lives, simply because she was the one in the home on a constant and continual basis.

Job 1:3... 'seven thousand sheep'

Mrs. Job would be the one on the home front when it came to supplying the community with dairy products (milk and milk by products).

Mrs. Job made sure the community food pantry was well stocked.

Mrs. Job supplied clothes for the homeless.

Job being CEO of his company, Mrs. Job would be second in command and the contact person when animals were needed for sacrifice and for food.

Mrs. Job would sign the order sheet and give instructions for the delivery.

When rams skins and horns needed replacing in the tabernacle, Mrs. Job would make sure only the most perfect instruments were used.

Mrs. Job would supervise and approve the new fabric textures and colors for the current and approaching seasons.

Mrs. Job was a trendsetter.

She would set the trend like Mrs. Eisenhower did with the hat that sat on top of the head.

Like the trend Jacqueline Kennedy set with the pillbox hat and the flip hairstyle.

When you desired festal/festive garments and robes you would go to Mrs. Job's boutique.

Preparing for weddings (weeklong celebrations) and clothing to attend festivals see Mrs. Job.

In today's setting Mrs. Job would run the designer shops for St. John's, Bob Mackie, Clara of New York, Donna Karan, Giorgio Armani and Vera Wang, to mention a few.

For the men's haberdashery the attire would include Hugo Bass, Brioni, Lord and Taylor and Ralph Lauren for Tuxedo and formal wear.

Mr. and Mrs. Job probably didn't wear the same outfit twice.

Mrs. Job would be the featured model (showing her personal wardrobe) in the fashion shows.

I imagine the children's wardrobe was extensive.

When winds, storms or fire destroyed someone's housing, Mrs. Job would arrange for the skins and tarpaulin for shelter.

Mrs. Job knew everyone and their family that was employed by her husband and would be certain that the families were provided for.

'and three thousand camels'

Mrs. Job made sure that there was an adequate amount of heavy cloaks for the shepherds and herdsmen. Mind you she did not physically fashion the cloaks, but made sure these items were furnished.

She could travel long distances with her friends to festivals, holy convocations and conventions.

For apostolic and prophetic gatherings held far away, Mrs. Job would make certain travel arrangements were secured.

No problem in transportation attending family reunions/celebrations and taking all the children.

The camels were the UPS of today, to send birthday, anniversary and celebration gifts.

'and five hundred yoke of oxen'

When it was time to harvest the land, Mrs. Job was generous about leaving more than the outside rows for gleaming.

In today's setting, Mrs. Job would supply food for the homeless shelters, halfway houses and group homes.

Mrs. Job would establish the grocery store chains and be asked to cut the ribbon at the openings.

She would store surplus food in the many warehouses constructed for the overflow.

'and five hundred she asses'

In today's picture when the president came to town, Mr. and

Mrs. Job would furnish the limousines.

When Kings and Queens visited the land, the Jobs' would be one of the host families.

There were many celebrations among the elite. Attending weddings, anniversaries, and newborn babies ceremonies were lengthy and distance was a factor. The limousine services of the Old Testament were the she asses owned by the Job's.

Whether it was the president or the mayor's breakfast for National Day of Prayer, Mrs. Job along with her husband was on the 'A' list of attendees and seated on the dais.

Mrs. Job would be the keynote speaker at the women's annual prayer breakfast and she would use her own transportation to arrive in style.

MRS. JOB'S TRAVAIL

Job 1:14,15....
'and five hundred yoke of oxen'

The land that was tilled and plowed by the oxen would now stand still and not produce a harvest.

In today's society Mrs. Job could no longer stock the homeless shelters or the food banks with groceries. At festivals and times of celebrations she would not be able to supply the fruit and vegetable trays.

Her ministry to provide food baskets to the homeless shelters and/or feed the widows and orphans in the community now ended. The institutions similar to Meijer's, Kroger's, Farmer Jacks and Piggly Wiggly, closed down.

Mrs. Job did not understand what was going on in her husband's life, the same as he did not understand.

There would be no more ribbon cutting ceremonies or the opening of new food chain stores.

It was as terrible for the Jobs' as the economic crash in America in 1929.

Job did not commit suicide.

Mrs. Job did not run away to escape their misery.

Her faith in God was as strong as his.

She stayed with her husband.

Job 1:16... 'seven thousand sheep'

When the sheep were consumed by fire from heaven, Mrs. Job also had a concern with milk and food for their household and their children, servants and their families. The clothing store chain would eventually go bankrupt.

You see, Mrs. Job had been the trendsetter in fashions.

The ladies of the community that came to her for advice on clothing and accessories avoided her now. She had lost her desire to wear her St. John's and Versage'.

Her designer shops folded, Bob Mackie, Harve Bernard, Kasper, Jacqueline Ferrar, and Oleg Cassini. Before the catastrophe, Mr. and Mrs. Job did not wear the same outfit twice.

Mrs. Job would not be introducing the latest style in shawls, tunics and robes. When the ladies of the community wanted to see a display of the newest designs of rugs and blankets for the home, they would seek Mrs. Job for her insight, up till now.

When the women needed to intercede for their husbands/families in times of mishap, Mrs. Job was the one to contact. Now these same ladies came together to pray for her.

If someone's crop failed or their stock was taken, see Mrs. Job for her to counsel with her husband on the injured's behalf. The tables had turned and someone was interceding for the Job's.

Mrs. Job had set up an outreach center to feed and clothe (with what was left in reserve) the widows and orphans left in their service.

Blankets were very important in this culture. The custom was that families would strip before going to bed and wrap up in blanket's and outdoor cloaks to keep warm during the night.

When winds and storms or fire destroyed someone's housing, Mrs. Job would arrange for the skins and tarpaulin for shelter, now a thing of the past.

No more utensils for the covering or furnishing for the tabernacle.

She not only lost the material things, she had the moral responsibility of taking care of those that depended on the Jobs' for basic needs.

Once their surplus was depleted, her outreach center would close down.

Mrs. Job lost as much as her husband.

Job 1:17... 'And three thousand camels'

Mrs. Job was no longer able to send birthday, wedding, or anniversary gifts to family and friends. Their camels were the UPS of today. She could no longer visit a relative that lived a long distance away whenever she wanted, or attend special occasions. Their camels were transportation to the feasts and royal celebrations. In today's language no more convocations or Apostolic and Prophetic gatherings that were held far away.

Job 1:18,19... 'Job's sons and daughters'

Mrs. Job lost her sons and her daughters as well as Job.

The children that came for the loins of Job were issued out of Mrs. Job's womb.

History records in the Old Testament that when one died, the grieving families prepared an elaborate weeklong observance.

The Bible states... *'Then Job arose, and rent his mantle, and shaved his head, and fell down upon the ground, and worshipped, (Job 1:20)'*

Mrs. Job must have tore at her clothes at the same time Job rent his mantle.

Mrs. Job would have put on sackcloth at the same time Job put on sackcloth.

Mrs. Job worshipped at the same time Job worshipped.

Mrs. Job went to the site of the disaster along with Job.

Mrs. Job accompanied her husband to search for their sons and daughters through the wreckage and ruins to prepare for a proper burial.

Mrs. Job assisted Job in discovering the remains of their children.

History also records that the bereaved families and friends of the families would come together to assemble around the deceased and indulge in lamentations.

Sometimes the gatherings bordered on hysteria.

Mr. and Mrs. Job were probably hysterical.

The men shaved off their hair and beards, and even brought blood by scratching themselves in paroxysms of grief.

The Israelites did not practice cremation or embalming, so burials were immediate.

Mrs. Job helped clean and prepare their children for decent burials.

Mrs. Job would have brought with her burial clothing for the children.

Mrs. Job assisted in fully clothing the remains and helping in the burial of the children.

It was customary to bury without a coffin.

The funeral party would take the deceased to the grave.

Mrs. Job was in that funeral party.

The gravesite could either be inside the city walls or in the courtyard of the house.

The ideal burial would be in a family vault that only the wealthy could afford.

Being a wealthy family, there was probably a family burial vault.

Mrs. Job would have chosen a variety of everyday objects such as weapons and jewelry and left them with their children in the family vault.

Fasting was practiced during the weeklong ceremony and was broken only by the funeral feast.

Mr. and Mrs. Job would have observed the fast.

It was customary to hold the funeral feast at the tomb itself on the day of burial.

Mrs. Job attended the funeral feast, but how do you eat after burying all your children?

It was normal to call in professional mourners to assist the family with their dirges (mournful chants).

Mr. and Mrs. Job needed no assistance.

Mrs. Job's insides must have been ripped apart. Her heart felt torn out.

Her arms ached to embrace their children once more.

How she grieved for her children, the way any mother grieves for her children.

Mrs. Job could make no more sense of what was happening than Job could.

Job 2:7... *'Job smote with boils'*

Job's body being wrecked with pain, with acute infectious disease of the skin, took a potsherd (fragments of baked broken clay vessels) to scrape the sores and boils on his body.

There were areas of his body that he could not reach or bear to scrape because of the pain.

Mrs. Job sat with Job in the ashes.

Mrs. Job scraped the areas he could not reach.

Mrs. Job was there all the time with Job.

Mrs. Job shared every pain Job experienced.

She wet his brow to calm the fever.

Consistent faith held their belief together solidly in the faithfulness of God.

This is the Scripture that I promised to share with you in an earlier chapter. It is from the Septuagint, the oldest Greek translation of the Hebrew Old Testament. This translation is based on an early fourth century manuscript.

> *Job 2:7,8... 'And when much time had passed, his wife said to him, How long wilt thou hold out, saying, Behold, I wait yet a little while, expecting the hope of my deliverance? for, behold, thy memorial is abolished from the earth, even thy sons and*

daughters, the pangs and pains of my womb which I bore in vain with sorrows; and thou thyself sittest down to spend the nights in the open air among the corruption of worms, and I am a wanderer and a servant from place to place and house to house, waiting for the setting of the sun, that I may rest from my labours and my pangs which now beset me: but say some word against the Lord, and die.'
(The Septuagint Version)

Mrs. Job put herself in harm's way with God when she spoke those words Job. She knew the relationship that Job had with God. She was not rational in her state of grief.

That statement seems to be a compassionate plea from one spouse to another.

Mrs. Job was out of her mind with pain and sorrow.

Mrs. Job's womb ached.

The reality and acceptance of the lost of their children, has set her to wandering and searching for a place to rest from her labours and pangs that now tormented her.

Mrs. Job knew that her husband could not commit suicide, because it was against God's Law.

Mrs. Job knew that she could not put him out of his physical misery because that too was against the Law of God.

Her proposal was spoken out of her emotions.

Her compassion for her husband was great.

She truly did not want to see him suffer anymore.

Mrs. Job suffered spiritually and emotionally along with Job.

Those closest to Job during his season of prosperity were nowhere to be found during his season of ruination. *(Job 19:13-19).*

JOB'S RESTORATION

Job 42:7,8... 'And it was so, that after the LORD had spoken these words unto Job, the LORD said to Eliphaz the Temanite, My wrath is kindled against thee, and against thy two friends: for ye have not spoken of me the thing that is right, as my servant Job hath. Therefore take unto you now seven bullocks and seven rams, and go to my servant Job, and offer up for yourselves a burnt offering; and my servant Job shall pray for you: for him will I accept: lest I deal with you after your folly, in that ye have not spoken of me the thing which is right, like my servant Job.'

When the LORD chasten Job's friends, He did not include Mrs. Job.

Being a just God, I believe he would not have left her out of offering up a sacrifice if He thought that she had spoken wrong to

His servant Job.

Job was not asked to offer up a sacrifice for Mrs. Job.

Job was not asked to pray for Mrs. Job.

It seems to me Mrs. Job was still in good standing with God.

If Mrs. Job's words or attitude had not been acceptable to God the same as Job's friends words were not acceptable, I believe God would have addressed that issue.

He did not make mention of Mrs. Job's remarks.

> ***Job 42:10… 'And the LORD turned the captivity of Job, when he prayed for his friends: also the LORD gave Job twice as much as he had before.'***

I underlined a portion of verse ten to highlight what is required of us when our friends and/or acquaintances have issues against us. God will cause those situations in our lives to turn around.

It is to HIM we turn.

God's wisdom in these times establishes in our understanding that He is in all of our circumstances.

Job 42:10

Job received double for his trouble. Gob blessed him with twice as much as he had before.

Mrs. Job received double for her trouble.

Job's brothers and sisters, his acquaintances and all that had been close to him before his calamities did eat bread with him in his house (his house was not harmed or destroyed).

They brought him gifts of money and gold earrings. (Job 42:11)

Job 42:12... 'fourteen thousand sheep'

Job was once again able to supply animals for the sacrificial system at the tabernacle.

His milk and flesh products were plentiful.

His clothing and textile business also thrived.

Mrs. Job regained her status in the community.

Mrs. Job's ministry for clothing the naked, feeding the hungry and stocking the food pantry was again on target.

Mrs. Job's designer shops reopened.

Mrs. Job's clothing store chains were reestablished.

The shepherds widows and orphans needs were met.

'six thousand camels'

The UPS of today was rolling again.

Long distance travel resumed.

Communication lines are open once more.

Mrs. Job reconnects with her family and friends far away.

Mrs. Job's transportation restored for her and her friends to annual feast and royal celebrations.

'and 1,000 yoke (2,000) of oxen'

Once again the land was plowed and tilled and an abundant harvest was expected. Homeless shelters would have plenty of nutritional food and the food banks stocked to overflowing.

Food chains reopened and more were established because of the double blessing.

Mrs. Job was busy with ribbon cuttings and celebrations.

'And 1,000 she asses'

Visiting of relatives that live far away was rekindled.

Mrs. Job was able to attend wedding, anniversaries and week long new baby celebrations.

Mr. and Mrs. Job were able to supply kings, queens and princes with limousine service.

Mrs. Job was now able to accept invitations to speak at prayer breakfasts and spiritual gatherings because transportation to travel distances was plentiful.

> **Job 42:13 'He had also seven sons and three daughters.'**

The sons and daughters that Job fathered after he was restored were issued through the same birth canal that the first set of children came through, Mrs. Job.

> **Job 42:14 'And he called the name of the first, Jemima (a dove); and the name of the second, Kezia (Cassia-A fragrance); and the name of the third, Kerenhappuch (Beautifier).**

There is no mention of Job having a second wife.
Mrs. Job gave birth to 20 children.

Mrs. Job was pregnant 180 months of her life.

That equals to 15 years of her life.

Mrs. Job went through deaths doorway 20 times in child delivery.

MRS. JOB WAS A REMARKABLE WOMAN.

I have examined extensively Mrs. Job, her husband, her children, and the natural side of her life. However, there is a powerful spiritual view to consider. All of the above possessions were a result of, and rewards for the godly life she lived and the deeply personal relationship she had with God.

In *Genesis 15* when God promised Abram that he would be father of many nations, Sarai was in the mind of God.

When God talked to and made promises to Abram, Sarai was always included in the equation.

Hagar and Ishmael were the result of Sarai's proposition.

When God talked to Job, Mrs. Job was included in the equation.

Job was the son and grandson of godly parents and grandparents. Mrs. Job would have come from a similar background to marry Job.

They would have heard about the exodus from their parents, and the miracles God worked among the Israelites. From their youth they would have witnessed the sacrificial system and made to understand what it was all about and why it was necessary. They knew how and why to worship God. How to fear (reverence) God. The Jobs' material wealth was the blessing from obedience and the Spiritual principal of sowing and reaping.

MRS. JOB
THE VIRTUOUS WOMAN

Proverbs 31:10-31

> *10 Who can find a virtuous woman? For her price*
> *is far above rubies.*

Mrs. Job's worth to her husband and her family could not be measured in material wealth.

> *11 The heart of her husband doth safely trust in*
> *her, so that he shall have no need of spoil.*

Job felt very secure with Mrs. Job handling all the affairs of the business at home.

> *12 She will do him good and not evil all the days of*
> *her life.*

Her love, honor and respect for Job is shown by emotional affection, perpetually.

> *13 She seeketh wool, and flax, and worketh willingly with her hands.*

Mrs. Job supervised and approved the finest quality in fabric and textiles from the textile mills.

> *14 She is like the merchants' ships; she bringeth her food from afar.*

Mrs. Job made certain that all provisions (no matter how far she had to go) for her family was plentiful. She took particular concern for the hungry, the naked and the homeless.

> *15 She riseth also while it is yet night, and giveth meat to her household, and a portion to her maidens.*

Mrs. Job's heartfelt responsibility to those that were in their employment, was of great concern to her and they were not an afterthought when it came to providing for them. Her concern was not only for their physical health and well being, but also for their strength regarding their working ability.

> *16 She considereth a field, and buyeth it: with the fruit of her hands she planteth a vineyard.*

On her travels, when Mrs. Job seen property or anything of value where she could invest and expect a return on her acquisition, she had the purchasing power. She conducts herself so that her husband has complete confidence in her. She considers the advantage it will be to the family.

> ***17 She girdeth her loins with strength, and strengtheneth her arms.***

The source of her strength, and the strength of her life was her God, so she was well able to strengthen those around.

> ***18 She preceiveth that her merchandise is good: her candle goeth not out by night.***

Mrs. Job was secure in sharing her talents and gifts to produce a good product that would bring a good price.

> ***19 She layeth her hands to the spindle, and her hands hold the distaff.***

Mrs. Job did not consider herself to good to work with her hands and create masterpieces.

> ***20 She stretcheth out her hands to the poor; yea, she reacheth forth her hands to the needy.***

Mrs. Job had a compassionate heart for those less fortunate than her. She understood her Christian and moral responsibility to reach out to the poor and needy. She liberally provided for the widows and orphans.

> *21 She is not afraid of the snow for her household:*
> *for all her household are clothed with scarlet.*

Weather posed no problem for her or her household because they had more than enough of the cloaks, shawls and tunics made from the ram's skin and camel hair. The color scarlet makes a good appearance.

> *22 She maketh herself coverings of tapestry; her*
> *clothing is silk and purple.*

She wears her clothes well, and the robes that her husband wears look better and wear better than anything purchased because she personally supervises the spinning for her and her husband's apparel. The silk refers to fine linen and the color purple denotes royalty.

> *23 Her husband is known in the gates, when he*
> *sitteth among the elders of the land.*

Men that sat in the gates were known to have good wives. They generally had cheerful countenance's and gentle ways. Their pleasant humor states that they have a good wife at home that takes care of them and their households.

**24 She maketh fine linen, and selleth it; and deliv-
ereth girdles unto the merchant.**

When Mrs. Job's staff had abundantly provided for her household, the surplus is sent to marketplaces and to other trading cities to make a profit.

**25 Strength and honor are her clothing; and she
shall rejoice in time to come.**

She is not gripped with fear. She had a sound mind and firmness in her decisions.

Mrs. Job had the resolve to endure many obstacles and disappointments. Her firmness and soundness are her strength and honor. She will experience times of pleasure and fullness of joy.

**26 She openeth her mouth with wisdom; and in her
tongue is the law of kindness.**

In her home she dispenses wise counsel to the community the same as Job does in the gate where he sits as a judge. Mrs. Job may be the weaker vessel but she is made strong by her wisdom. She is discreet and trustworthy. When she does speak, it is with purpose.

**27 She looketh well to the ways of her household,
and eateth not the bread of idleness.**

Mrs. Job takes care of her family/household needs. She was not idle or useless when she was young and she is not idle or useless now.

> **28 Her children arise up, and call her blessed; her husband also, and he praiseth her.**

Her children were dutiful and respectful to her. They followed her Christian example as they grew up in a nurturing environment. Her husband is happy in her and takes every opportunity to speak well of her.

> **29 Many daughters have done virtuously, but thou excellest them all.**

A woman that fears the Lord, shall have praise of God (Romans 2:29). Her husband, children and neighbors praise her. The favor of God rest upon her.

> **30 Favor is deceitful, and beauty is vain: but a woman that feareth the LORD, she shall be praised.**

Mrs. Job's crowning glory and completeness is in the fact that she fears (loves) the Lord. In her heart reigns the reverence for God and it is precious in His sight. The law of love and kindness is written in her heart.

31 Give her of the fruit of her hands; and let her
own works praise her in the gates.

Her good works will proclaim her praise. She reaps the benefits of the fruit of her body and her hands, her children, household. If no one ever acknowledges her, her own works will proclaim and praise her.

MRS. JOB

THE TRUE VIRTUOUS WOMAN

CPSIA information can be obtained at www.ICGtesting.com
Printed in the USA
BVOW05s0255020415

394361BV00003B/29/P